Standard Grade | Credit

Chemistry

Leckie✕Leckie

First exam published in 2000.

Published by Leckie & Leckie, 8 Whitehill Terrace, St. Andrews, Scotland KY16 8RN tel: 01334 475656 fax: 01334 477392 enquiries@leckieandleckie.co.uk www.leckieandleckie.co.uk

Leckie & Leckie Project Team: Andrea Collington; Peter Dennis; Bruce Ryan

ISBN 1-84372-191-0

A CIP Catalogue record for this book is available from the British Library.

Printed in Scotland by Scotprint.

Leckie & Leckie is a division of Granada Learning Limited, part of ITV plc.

Acknowledgements

Every effort has been made to trace the copyright holders and to obtain their permission for the use of copyright material. Leckie & Leckie will gladly receive information enabling them to rectify any error or omission in subsequent editions.

2000 CREDIT

C

FOR OFFICIAL USE

	KU	PS
Total Marks		

0500/402

NATIONAL
QUALIFICATIONS
2000

MONDAY, 22 MAY
10.50 AM – 12.20 PM

**CHEMISTRY
STANDARD GRADE**
Credit Level

Fill in these boxes and read what is printed below.

Full name of centre

Town

Forename(s)

Surname

Date of birth
Day Month Year   Scottish candidate number   Number of seat

1 All questions should be attempted.

2 Necessary data will be found in the Data Booklet provided for Chemistry at Standard Grade and Intermediate 2.

3 The questions may be answered in any order but all answers are to be written in this answer book, and must be written clearly and legibly in ink.

4 Rough work, if any should be necessary, as well as the fair copy, is to be written in this book.

Rough work should be scored through when the fair copy has been written.

5 Additional space for answers and rough work will be found at the end of the book.

6 The size of the space provided for an answer should not be taken as an indication of how much to write. It is not necessary to use all the space.

7 Before leaving the examination room you must give this book to the invigilator. If you do not, you may lose all the marks for this paper.

**SCOTTISH
QUALIFICATIONS
AUTHORITY**

PART 1

In Questions 1 to 8 of this part of the paper, an answer is given by circling the appropriate letter (or letters) in the answer grid provided.

In some questions, two letters are required for full marks.

If more than the correct number of answers is given, marks will be deducted.

In some cases, the number of correct responses is NOT identified in the question.

A total of 20 marks is available in this part of the paper.

SAMPLE QUESTION

A CH_4	B H_2	C CO_2
D CO	E C_2H_5OH	F C

(a) Identify the hydrocarbon(s).

Ⓐ	B	C
D	E	F

The one correct answer to part (a) is A. This should be circled.

(b) Identify the **two** elements.

A	Ⓑ	C
D	E	Ⓕ

As indicated in this question, there are **two** correct answers to part (b). These are B and F. Both answers are circled.

(c) Identify the substance(s) which can burn to produce **both** carbon dioxide and water.

Ⓐ	B	C
D	Ⓔ	F

There are **two** correct answers to part (c). These are A and E. Both answers are circled.

If, after you have recorded your answer, you decide that you have made an error and wish to make a change, you should cancel the original answer and circle the answer you now consider to be correct. Thus, in part (a), if you want to change an answer A to an answer D, your answer sheet would look like this:

A̶	B	C
Ⓓ	E	F

If you want to change back to an answer which has already been scored out, you should enter a tick (✓) in the box of the answer of your choice, thus:

✓A̶	B	C
D̶	E	F

1. The grid shows the symbols for some elements.

A		B		C	
	Al		Na		P
D		E		F	
	Mg		O		Ba

You may wish to use page 1 of the data booklet to help you.

(a) Identify the **two** elements which have atoms with the same number of outer electrons.

A	B	C
D	E	F

(b) Identify the **two** elements which react to form a covalent compound.

A	B	C
D	E	F

(c) Identify the **two** elements which form an ionic compound with a formula of the type X_2Y, where X is a metal.

A	B	C
D	E	F

[Turn over

KU	PS

2. Carbohydrates are formed in plants.

A	glucose
B	maltose
C	sucrose
D	starch
E	fructose

(a) Identify the **two** carbohydrates with formula $C_{12}H_{22}O_{11}$.

A
B
C
D
E

(b) Identify the carbohydrate which does **not** react with either iodine solution or Benedict's solution.

A
B
C
D
E

KU	PS

3. Hydrocarbon compounds have many uses.

A	B

CH_3 H
  | |
  C = C
  | |
  H CH_3
	CH_3 H
	  | |
	H − C — C − H
	  | |
	  H H

C	D

CH_3 H
  | |
H − C — C − H
  | |
  H CH_3
	CH_3 H
	  | |
	  C = C
	  | |
	  H H

(a) Identify the hydrocarbon which is used to make poly(butene).

A	B
C	D

(b) Identify the hydrocarbon which is an isomer of

```
     H     H
      \   /
       C
   H   / \   H
    \ /   \ /
     C  —  C
    /       \
   H         H
```

A	B
C	D

[Turn over

Official SQA Past Papers: Credit Chemistry 2000

DO NOT
WRITE IN
THIS
MARGIN

KU | PS

4. A bromide ion is formed when a bromine atom gains one electron.
   Identify the true statement(s) about this change.

A	The change represents reduction.
B	The atomic number increases by one.
C	The particle becomes negatively charged.
D	The number of electron energy levels increases by one.
E	The bromide ion has the same electron arrangement as an argon atom.

A
B
C
D
E

5. There are different types of chemical reaction.

A	B	C
displacement	hydrolysis	fermentation
D	E	F
condensation	addition	redox

(a) Identify the type of reaction that occurs when glucose molecules join to form starch.

A	B	C
D	E	F

(b) Identify the type(s) of reaction represented by the following equation.

$$Fe(s) \quad + \quad Cu^{2+}SO_4^{2-}(aq) \quad \rightarrow \quad Cu(s) \quad + \quad Fe^{2+}SO_4^{2-}(aq)$$

A	B	C
D	E	F

[Turn over

Official SQA Past Papers: Credit Chemistry 2000

DO NOT
WRITE IN
THIS
MARGIN

KU | PS

6. A gas pipeline made from iron can be protected by attaching scrap magnesium.

Identify the correct statement(s).

A	The magnesium would be oxidised.
B	The magnesium would not corrode.
C	The iron would corrode faster than the magnesium.
D	The magnesium would provide sacrificial protection.
E	Electrons would flow from the iron to the magnesium.

A
B
C
D
E

7. The grid below shows pairs of chemicals.

A	B
Mg(s) + HCl(aq)	NaOH(aq) + H_2SO_4(aq)
C	D
Cu(s) + H_2SO_4(aq)	Zn(s) + $AgNO_3$(aq)
E	F
$CuSO_4$(aq) + Na_2CO_3(aq)	$CaCO_3$(s) + HCl(aq)

(*a*) Identify the pair(s) which would react to produce water.

A	B
C	D
E	F

(*b*) Identify the pair which would **not** react.

A	B
C	D
E	F

[Turn over

8. Hydrochloric acid and sulphuric acid are two common laboratory acids.

A	Equal numbers of positive and negative ions are present.
B	A precipitate would be produced with barium hydroxide solution.
C	The H^+ ion concentration would increase when water was added.
D	Electrolysis would produce hydrogen gas at the negative electrode.
E	1 mole of sodium hydroxide would be neutralised by 0·5 moles of the acid.

(a) Identify the statement which can be applied to **both** dilute sulphuric acid and dilute hydrochloric acid.

A
B
C
D
E

(b) Identify the statement(s) which can be applied to dilute sulphuric acid but **not** to dilute hydrochloric acid.

A
B
C
D
E

Marks | KU | PS

PART 2

A total of 40 marks is available in this part of the paper.

9. The uses of metals are related to their properties.

Metal	Density (g/cm^3)	Relative strength	Relative electrical conductivity
Aluminium	2·7	1·0	3·8
Steel	7·9	4·0	1·0
Copper	8·9	2·5	5·9

Overhead electricity cables have a steel core surrounded by an aluminium sheath.

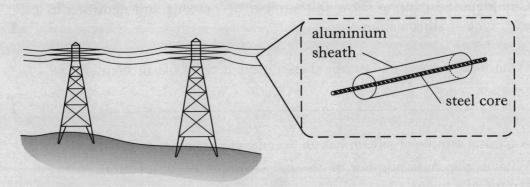

Using information from the table, suggest:

(a) an advantage of using aluminium rather than copper for the cable;

_____

_____

_____ 1

(b) why the cables have a steel core.

_____

_____

_____ 1

(2)

[Turn over

Marks | KU | PS

10. There are three different types of silicon atom.

Type of atom	Number of protons	Number of neutrons
$^{28}_{14}\text{Si}$		
$^{29}_{14}\text{Si}$		
$^{30}_{14}\text{Si}$		

(a) Complete the table to show the number of protons and neutrons in each type of silicon atom.

1

(b) What name is used to describe these different types of silicon atom?

_____

1

(c) A natural sample of silicon has an average atomic mass of 28·11.

What is the mass number of the most common type of atom in the sample of silicon?

_____

1

(3)

11. Crude oil arriving at the BP refinery in Grangemouth is separated into different fractions.

Fraction and Boiling Range

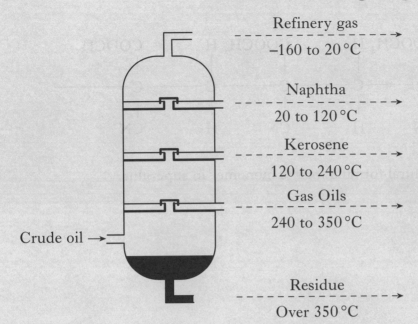

Refinery gas
−160 to 20 °C

Naphtha
20 to 120 °C

Kerosene
120 to 240 °C

Gas Oils
240 to 350 °C

Crude oil →

Residue
Over 350 °C

(a) In which fraction will pentane be found?
You may wish to use page 6 of the data booklet to help you.

_____   1

(b) Why is the gas oils fraction more viscous than the kerosene fraction?

_____

_____

_____   1

(c) Fractions which are surplus to requirements can be cracked.

(i) Give a reason for cracking fractions.

_____

_____

_____   1

(ii) A catalyst is used to speed up this process.
Suggest another reason for using a catalyst.

_____

_____

_____   1

Marks | KU | PS

12. When superglue sets a polymer is formed. The polymer has the following structure.

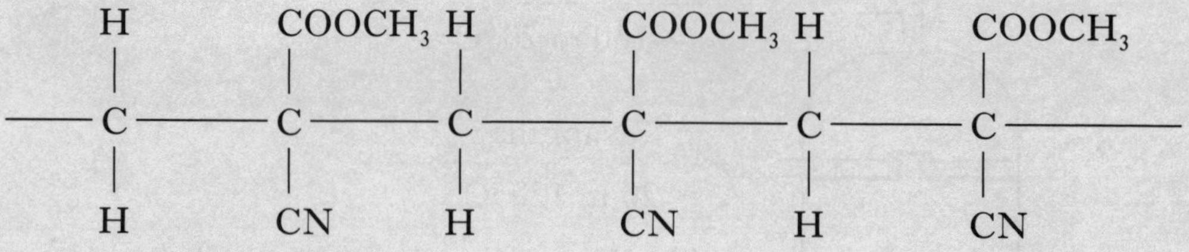

$$
\begin{array}{cccccc}
H & COOCH_3 & H & COOCH_3 & H & COOCH_3 \\
| & | & | & | & | & | \\
--C-- & --C-- & --C-- & --C-- & --C-- & --C-- \\
| & | & | & | & | & | \\
H & CN & H & CN & H & CN
\end{array}
$$

(a) Draw the structural formula for the monomer in superglue.

1

(b) Name a toxic gas given off when superglue burns.

_____

1

(2)

Marks | KU | PS

13. Silicon is used in the electronics industry and exists naturally as silicon oxide. It can be extracted in the following way.

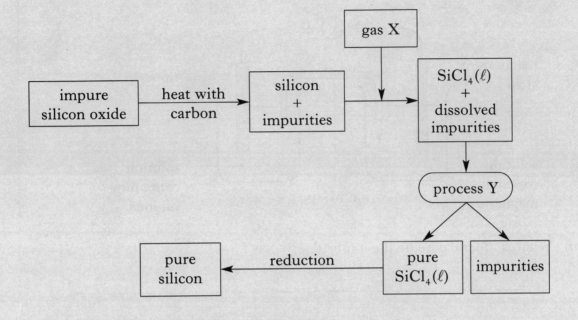

(a) Write the formula for silicon oxide.

_____

1

(b) Name gas X.

_____

1

(c) Name process Y.

_____

1

(d) Draw a diagram to show the **shape** of a $SiCl_4$ molecule.

1

(e) The equation for the reduction of $SiCl_4$ is:

$$SiCl_4 \quad + \quad H_2 \quad \rightarrow \quad Si \quad + \quad HCl$$

Balance this equation.

1

(5)

Marks   KU   PS

14. The diagram shows a cell which can produce electricity.

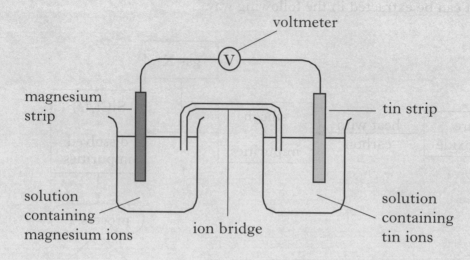

(a) What is the purpose of the ion bridge?

_____

_____   1

(b) Name a tin compound which could be used to make the solution containing tin ions.

You may wish to use page 5 of your data booklet to help you.

_____   1

(c) The following cell produces a higher voltage than the cell above.

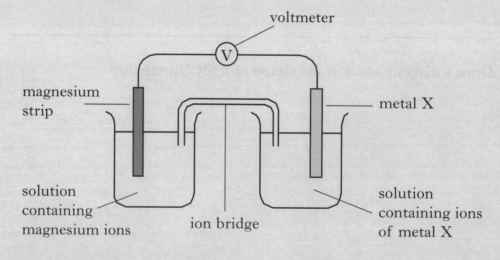

Suggest a name for metal X.

_____   1

(3)

15. The percentage of oxygen in air can be determined by reacting the oxygen with copper. The air is passed backwards and forwards over the heated copper.

Calculation:

$$\text{Percentage of oxygen in air} = \frac{\text{reduction in volume of air}}{\text{volume of air at start of experiment}} \times 100$$

The following is taken from a pupil's lab book.

volume of air at start of experiment	=	$60 \cdot 0 \, \text{cm}^3$
volume of gas at end of experiment	=	$47 \cdot 5 \, \text{cm}^3$

(a) Calculate the percentage of oxygen in the sample of air.
Show your working clearly.

Percentage of oxygen in air = _____ %

1

(b) Suggest a reason why the air is passed backwards and forwards over the heated copper.

_____

_____

_____

1

(c) Suggest a reason why carbon cannot be used in place of the copper.

_____

_____

_____

1

(3)

Marks | KU | PS

16. Acids can be shown to contain $H^+(aq)$ using a Hoffman voltameter.

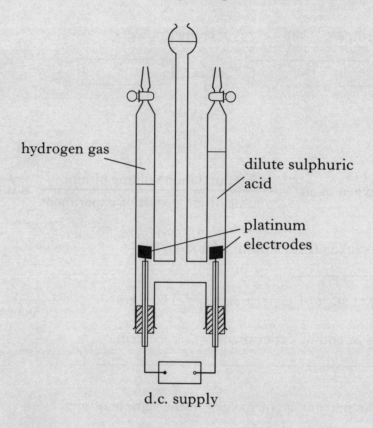

hydrogen gas

dilute sulphuric acid

platinum electrodes

d.c. supply

(a) Why must a d.c. supply be used?

_____

_____

_____   1

(b) The volume of hydrogen gas produced over a period of time was measured during the electrolysis of dilute sulphuric acid.

The results are shown in the table.

Time (min)	0	5	8	12	20
Volume of gas (cm³)	0	8·5	13·5	20·0	33·0

Official SQA Past Papers: Credit Chemistry 2000

DO NOT
WRITE IN
THIS
MARGIN

Marks | KU | PS

16. (*b*) **(continued)**

Draw a line graph of the results.

(Additional graph paper, if required, will be found on page 25.)

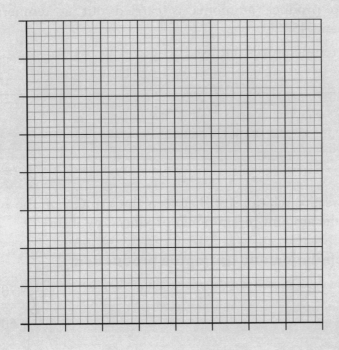

2

(*c*) Predict the volume of hydrogen gas which would be produced during the first 10 minutes.

_____ 1

(*d*) Write the ion-electron equation for the formation of hydrogen gas.

You may wish to use your data booklet to help you.

_____ 1

(5)

[Turn over

Marks | KU | PS

17. (a) Name the industrial process used to manufacture ammonia.

_____

1

(b) The reaction to produce ammonia is carried out at temperatures between 380 °C and 450 °C.

Why are higher temperatures not used?

_____

_____

_____

1

(c) The graph shows the relationship between the growth of the human population and the amount of ammonia produced by industry.

World population and ammonia production

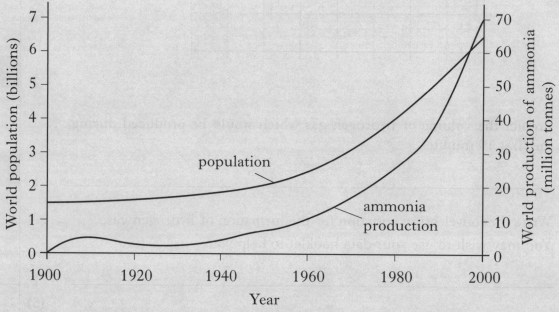

Why has the increase in world population led to an increase in ammonia production?

_____

_____

_____

1

(3)

Marks | KU | PS

18. Camping gas contains propane and butane.

Propane and butane are members of the alkane homologous series.

(a) What is meant by the term "homologous series"?

_____

_____

_____   **1**

(b) The equation for the burning of propane is

$$C_3H_8(g) \quad + \quad 5O_2(g) \quad \rightarrow \quad 3CO_2(g) \quad + \quad 4H_2O(g)$$

Calculate the mass of water produced when 22 g of propane burns.

Answer = _____ g   **2**

(3)

[Turn over

Marks | KU | PS

19. Visking tubing can be used to model the gut wall.

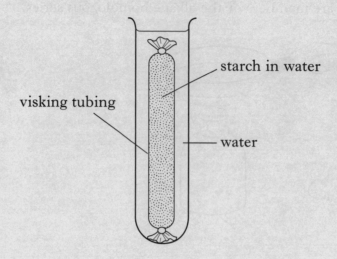

starch in water

visking tubing

water

(a) Describe how you would show that starch molecules are too large to pass through the visking tubing.

_____

_____

_____

1

(b) During digestion starch is hydrolysed by amylase.

(i) What is meant by "hydrolysed"?

_____

_____

1

DO NOT
WRITE IN
THIS
MARGIN

Marks | KU | PS

19. *(b)* **(continued)**

(ii) Using all the chemicals and apparatus below describe the experiment you would carry out to show that hydrolysed starch can pass through the visking tubing. (You may wish to draw a diagram.)

You may use other apparatus if required.

Chemicals and apparatus.

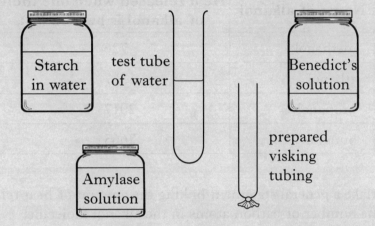

2

(4)

[Turn over for Question 20 on *Page twenty-four*

Marks | KU | PS

20. (*a*) Yeast can be used to convert carbohydrates to ethanol.

What name is given to this process?

_____ **1**

(*b*) Ethanol is the second member of the alkanol family.

The combustion of an alkanol releases heat energy.

Name of alkanol	Heat released when one mole of alkanol is burned (kJ)
methanol	726
ethanol	1367
propanol	2017
butanol	2665

(i) Make a general statement linking the amount of heat released and the number of carbon atoms in the alkanol molecule.

_____

_____

_____ **1**

(ii) Predict the amount of heat released, when 1 mole of pentanol burns.

_____ kJ **1**

(3)

[*END OF QUESTION PAPER*]

ADDITIONAL SPACE FOR ANSWERS

ADDITIONAL GRAPH PAPER FOR QUESTION 16(*b*)

DO NOT
WRITE IN
THIS
MARGIN

KU PS

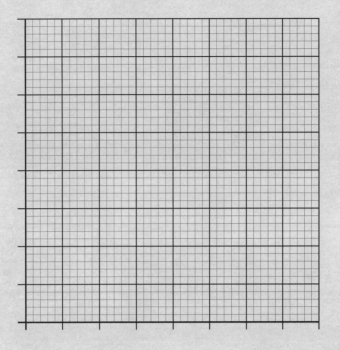

ADDITIONAL SPACE FOR ANSWERS

2001 CREDIT

C

FOR OFFICIAL USE

	KU	PS
Total Marks		

0500/402

NATIONAL
QUALIFICATIONS
2001

THURSDAY, 24 MAY
10.50 AM – 12.20 PM

CHEMISTRY
STANDARD GRADE
Credit Level

Fill in these boxes and read what is printed below.

Full name of centre

Town

Forename(s)

Surname

Date of birth
Day Month Year

Scottish candidate number

Number of seat

1 All questions should be attempted.

2 Necessary data will be found in the Data Booklet provided for Chemistry at Standard Grade and Intermediate 2.

3 The questions may be answered in any order but all answers are to be written in this answer book, and must be written clearly and legibly in ink.

4 Rough work, if any should be necessary, as well as the fair copy, is to be written in this book.

   Rough work should be scored through when the fair copy has been written.

5 Additional space for answers and rough work will be found at the end of the book.

6 The size of the space provided for an answer should not be taken as an indication of how much to write. It is not necessary to use all the space.

7 Before leaving the examination room you must give this book to the invigilator. If you do not, you may lose all the marks for this paper.

SCOTTISH
QUALIFICATIONS
AUTHORITY

MCB 0500/402 6/3/26420

PART 1

In Questions 1 to 9 of this part of the paper, an answer is given by circling the appropriate letter (or letters) in the answer grid provided.

In some questions, two letters are required for full marks.

If more than the correct number of answers is given, marks will be deducted.

In some cases, the number of correct responses is NOT identified in the question.

A total of 20 marks is available in this part of the paper.

SAMPLE QUESTION

A	B	C
CH_4	H_2	CO_2
D	**E**	**F**
CO	C_2H_5OH	C

(a) Identify the hydrocarbon(s).

Ⓐ	B	C
D	E	F

The one correct answer to part (a) is A. This should be circled.

(b) Identify the **two** elements.

A	Ⓑ	C
D	E	Ⓕ

As indicated in this question, there are **two** correct answers to part (b). These are B and F. Both answers are circled.

(c) Identify the substance(s) which can burn to produce **both** carbon dioxide and water.

Ⓐ	B	C
D	Ⓔ	F

There are **two** correct answers to part (c). These are A and E.

Both answers are circled.

If, after you have recorded your answer, you decide that you have made an error and wish to make a change, you should cancel the original answer and circle the answer you now consider to be correct. Thus, in part (a), if you want to change an answer A to an answer D, your answer sheet would look like this:

A̶	B	C
Ⓓ	E	F

If you want to change back to an answer which has already been scored out, you should enter a tick (✓) in the box of the answer of your choice, thus:

✓A̶	B	C
D̶	E	F

1. Iron can be coated with different materials which provide a physical barrier against corrosion.

A	tin
B	grease
C	paint
D	plastic
E	zinc

(a) Identify the coating which also provides sacrificial protection.

A
B
C
D
E

(b) Identify the coating which, if scratched, would cause the iron to rust faster than normal.

A
B
C
D
E

[Turn over

2. Frank and Dave carried out several experiments with metals and acids.

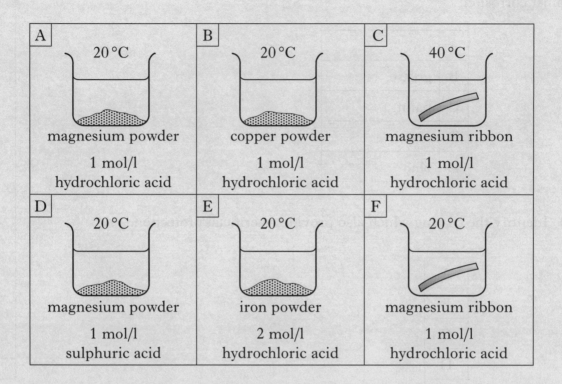

A	B	C
20 °C	20 °C	40 °C
magnesium powder	copper powder	magnesium ribbon
1 mol/l hydrochloric acid	1 mol/l hydrochloric acid	1 mol/l hydrochloric acid

D	E	F
20 °C	20 °C	20 °C
magnesium powder	iron powder	magnesium ribbon
1 mol/l sulphuric acid	2 mol/l hydrochloric acid	1 mol/l hydrochloric acid

(a) Identify the **two** experiments which should be compared to show the effect of particle size on reaction rate.

A	B	C
D	E	F

(b) Identify the experiment in which no reaction would take place.

A	B	C
D	E	F

3.

A	B	C
$^{24}_{11}Na$	$^{14}_{6}C$	$^{19}_{9}F$
D	E	F
$^{24}_{12}Mg^{2+}$	$^{19}_{9}F^{-}$	$^{12}_{6}C$

(a) Identify the **two** particles with the same number of neutrons.

A	B	C
D	E	F

(b) Identify the **two** atoms which are isotopes.

A	B	C
D	E	F

(c) Identify the **two** particles with the same electron arrangement as neon.

A	B	C
D	E	F

[Turn over

Official SQA Past Papers: Credit Chemistry 2001

DO NOT
WRITE IN
THIS
MARGIN

KU PS

4. The equations represent chemical reactions involving carbohydrates.

A	carbon dioxide + water → glucose + oxygen
B	glucose → starch + water
C	starch + water → glucose
D	glucose → ethanol + carbon dioxide
E	glucose + oxygen → carbon dioxide + water

(a) Identify the reaction which is catalysed by enzymes in yeast.

A
B
C
D
E

(b) Identify the hydrolysis reaction.

A
B
C
D
E

(c) Identify the reaction which takes place in animals during respiration.

A
B
C
D
E

KU | PS

5. The grid shows the names of some chemical compounds.

A	B	C
sodium hydroxide	potassium nitrate	sodium chloride
D	E	F
lithium carbonate	sodium phosphate	barium sulphate

(a) Identify the **two** bases.

A	B	C
D	E	F

(b) Identify the compound which could be prepared by precipitation.
You may wish to refer to page 5 of the data booklet.

A	B	C
D	E	F

[Turn over

6. The grid contains information about the particles found in atoms.

A	B	C
relative mass = 1	charge = 1+	found inside the nucleus
D	E	F
charge = 1−	relative mass almost zero	charge = zero

Identify the term(s) which can be applied to **both** protons **and** neutrons.

A	B	C
D	E	F

7. Several conductivity experiments were carried out using the apparatus shown below.

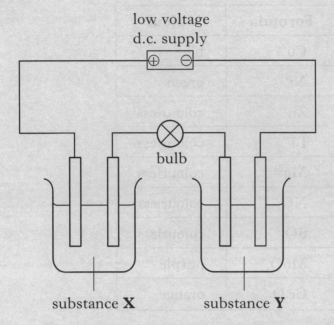

Identify the experiment(s) in which the bulb would light.

Experiment	Substance X	Substance Y
A	glucose solution	sodium chloride solution
B	molten tin	liquid mercury
C	sodium chloride solution	hexane
D	nickel bromide solution	molten sodium chloride
E	solid potassium nitrate	copper sulphate solution

A
B
C
D
E

[Turn over

Official SQA Past Papers: Credit Chemistry 2001

DO NOT
WRITE IN
THIS
MARGIN

KU | PS

8. The table below shows the names and colours of some common ions.

Ion	Formula	Colour
copper	Cu^{2+}	blue
nickel	Ni^{2+}	green
zinc	Zn^{2+}	colourless
lithium	Li^+	colourless
magnesium	Mg^{2+}	colourless
nitrate	NO_3^-	colourless
sulphate	SO_4^{2-}	colourless
permanganate	MnO_4^-	purple
dichromate	$Cr_2O_7^{2-}$	orange

Identify the true statement(s) based on the information in the table.

A	Copper nitrate is blue.
B	Coloured ions contain transition metals.
C	Ions containing oxygen are colourless.
D	All transition metal ions are coloured.
E	All lithium compounds are colourless.

A
B
C
D
E

9. To turn a gas into a liquid it must be cooled below a temperature known as its critical temperature.

Gas	Formula	Relative formula mass	Critical temperature/°C
hydrogen	H_2	2	−240
helium	He	4	−268
ammonia	NH_3	17	133
oxygen	O_2	32	−119
carbon dioxide	CO_2	44	31

Identify the true statement(s) based on the information in the table.

A	Compounds have higher critical temperatures than elements.
B	Critical temperature increases as relative formula mass increases.
C	Diatomic elements have higher critical temperatures than monatomic elements.
D	Carbon dioxide can be a liquid at 40 °C.

A
B
C
D

[Turn over

DO NOT WRITE IN THIS MARGIN

Marks | KU | PS

PART 2

A total of 40 marks is available in this part of the paper.

10. Andrew investigated the effect of different hydrocarbons on bromine solution.

Hydrocarbon	Formula	Effect on bromine solution
A	C_5H_{12}	
B	C_6H_{12}	no effect
C	C_5H_{10}	no effect
D	C_5H_{10}	quickly decolourised

(a) Complete the table to show the effect of hydrocarbon **A** on bromine solution.

1

(b) Name hydrocarbon **B**.

_____

1

(c) What term is used to describe a pair of hydrocarbons like **C** and **D**?

_____

1

(3)

Marks | KU | PS

11. Siobhan carried out some experiments with four metals (**W**, **X**, **Y** and **Z**) and some of their compounds. She made the following observations.

> When each metal was placed in cold water, only metal Y reacted.
>
> Only metal W was obtained from its oxide by heating.
>
> When metal X was placed in a solution containing ions of metal Z, metal X dissolved and solid metal Z was formed.

(a) Name the gas formed when metal **Y** reacts with water.

_____ 1

(b) Suggest names for metals **W** and **Y**.

metal **W** _____   metal **Y** _____ 1

(c) Place the four metals (**W**, **X**, **Y** and **Z**) in order of reactivity (most reactive first).

_____ 1

(d) Name the type of chemical reaction which takes place when a metal is extracted from its oxide.

_____ 1

(4)

[Turn over

Marks | KU | PS

12. Some sources of methane contain hydrogen sulphide (H_2S).
This is removed before the methane is used as a fuel.

(a) Balance the equation for the combustion of methane.

$$CH_4 \quad + \quad O_2 \quad \rightarrow \quad CO_2 \quad + \quad H_2O$$

1

(b) Why is hydrogen sulphide removed before the methane is used as a fuel?

_____

_____

_____

1

(c) Hydrogen sulphide is removed by reacting it with sulphur dioxide.

$$2H_2S \quad + \quad SO_2 \quad \rightarrow \quad 2H_2O \quad + \quad 3S$$

Calculate the mass of sulphur produced, in grams, when 34 g of hydrogen sulphide reacts with sulphur dioxide.

Show your working clearly.

2

12. (continued)

(d) The table shows the relationship between solubility of sulphur dioxide in water and the temperature of the water.

Temperature/°C	0	10	20	30	40	60	80
Solubility/ grams per litre	225	145	95	60	35	15	5

(i) Draw a line graph of solubility against temperature.

Use appropriate scales to fill most of the graph paper.

(Additional graph paper, if required, will be found on page 24.)

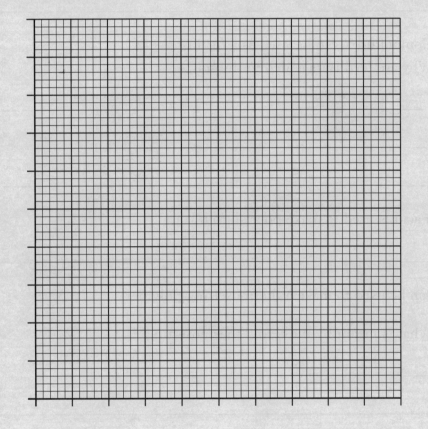

2

(ii) State the relationship between the solubility of sulphur dioxide in water and the temperature of the water.

_____

_____

1

(7)

[Turn over

Marks | KU | PS

13. Nitrogen forms many useful compounds.

Compound	Formula
Y	$(NH_4)_3PO_4$
potassium nitrate	KNO_3
urea	$CO(NH_2)_2$

(a) (i) Name compound **Y**.

_____   1

(ii) Compound **Y** can be used as a fertiliser.
Why are fertilisers added to the soil?

_____

_____

_____   1

(b) Which acid is used to make potassium nitrate?

_____   1

(c) Urea can be used to make a thermosetting polymer.

(i) What is meant by the term "thermosetting"?

_____

_____   1

(ii) Calculate the percentage mass of nitrogen in urea.
Show your working clearly.

2

(6)

Marks | KU | PS

14. The table compares the mass of ions found in ocean water with the mass of ions found in water from the Dead Sea.

Ion	Mass in 1 litre of ocean water/g	Mass in 1 litre of Dead Sea water/g
Na^+	10·7	31·5
K^+	0·4	6·8
Mg^{2+}	1·3	36·2
Ca^{2+}	0·4	13·4
Cl^-	19·2	183·0
Br^-	0·1	5·2
SO_4^{2-}	2·5	0·6

(a) What general statement can be made about the mass of ions in water from the Dead Sea compared with ocean water?

_____

_____

_____   1

(b) Suggest a name for a compound which might be obtained if a sample of water from the Dead Sea was evaporated to dryness.

_____   1

(c) Calculate the concentration of calcium ions, in mol/l, in ocean water.

1

(3)

[Turn over

Marks | KU | PS

15. Sarah set up the circuit shown below.

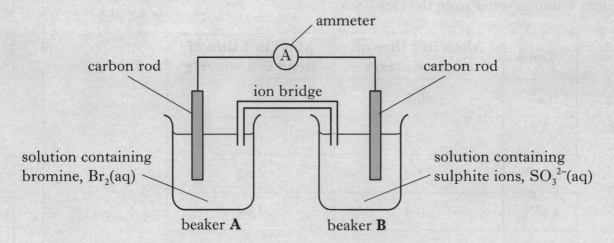

In beaker **B** sulphite ions are converted to sulphate ions:

$$SO_3^{2-}(aq) \quad + \quad H_2O(\ell) \quad \rightarrow \quad SO_4^{2-}(aq) \quad + \quad 2H^+(aq) \quad + \quad 2e^-$$

(a) On the diagram, clearly mark the path and the direction of the electron flow.

1

(b) (i) What term is used to describe the type of chemical reaction taking place in beaker **B**?

_____

1

(ii) Suggest what would happen to the pH in beaker **B**.

_____

1

(c) Write the ion-electron equation for the chemical reaction taking place in beaker **A**.

You may wish to use the data booklet to help you.

_____

1

(4)

DO NOT WRITE IN THIS MARGIN

Marks KU PS

16. (*a*) Ammonia is made industrially by the Haber process.

Name the catalyst used to make ammonia.

____ **1**

(*b*) Name **two** compounds, which can react together to produce ammonia in the laboratory.

____ **1**

(*c*) The atoms in an ammonia molecule are held together by covalent bonds. A covalent bond is a shared pair of electrons.

Explain how this holds the atoms together.

____

____

____

____

____ **1**

(3)

[Turn over

Marks | KU | PS

17. (a) Methoxyethane belongs to a homologous series of compounds called ethers.

What is meant by the term "homologous series"?

_____

_____

_____

1

(b) Methoxyethane is formed when bromomethane, ethanol and sodium react together.

$$2\ CH_3Br\ +\ 2\ C_2H_5OH\ +\ 2\ Na\ \rightarrow\ 2\ CH_3OC_2H_5\ +\ 2\ NaBr\ +\ \mathbf{X}_2$$
bromomethane   ethanol   methoxyethane

    (i) Name $\mathbf{X}_2$.

    _____

1

    (ii) Draw a **full** structural formula for methoxyethane ($CH_3OC_2H_5$).

1

(3)

Marks | KU | PS

18. Sea water contains magnesium ions. The diagram below shows how magnesium can be extracted from sea water.

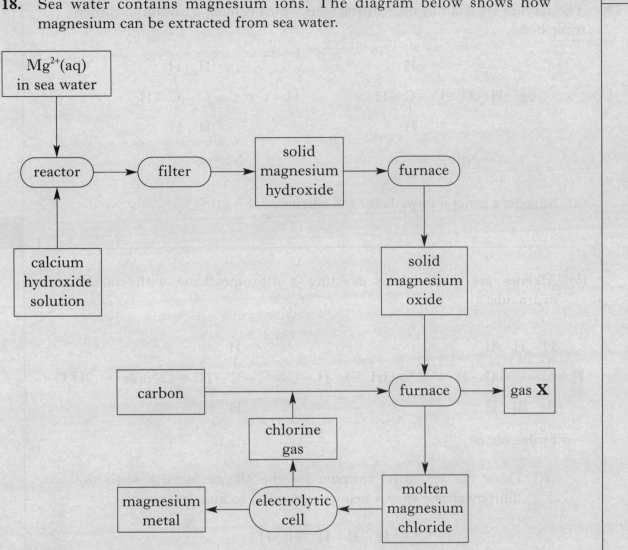

(a) Name the type of chemical reaction which takes place in the reactor.

_____ 1

(b) Write the **ionic** formula for calcium hydroxide.

_____ 1

(c) Name gas **X**.

_____ 1

(d) Why do ionic compounds like magnesium chloride conduct electricity when molten?

_____

_____

_____ 1

(4)

Marks   KU   PS

19. The alkynes are a family of hydrocarbons which contain a carbon to carbon triple bond.

eg
$$H-C\equiv C-\underset{\underset{H}{|}}{\overset{\overset{H}{|}}{C}}-H \qquad H-C\equiv C-\underset{\underset{H}{|}}{\overset{\overset{H}{|}}{C}}-\underset{\underset{H}{|}}{\overset{\overset{H}{|}}{C}}-H$$

  propyne   butyne

(a) Suggest a general formula for the alkynes.

_____   1

(b) Alkynes are prepared by reacting a dibromoalkane with sodium hydroxide.

$$H-\underset{\underset{Br}{|}}{\overset{\overset{H}{|}}{C}}-\underset{\underset{Br}{|}}{\overset{\overset{H}{|}}{C}}-\underset{\underset{H}{|}}{\overset{\overset{H}{|}}{C}}-H \ + \ 2NaOH \ \rightarrow \ H-C\equiv C-\underset{\underset{H}{|}}{\overset{\overset{H}{|}}{C}}-H \ + \ 2NaBr \ + \ 2H_2O$$

  dibromoalkane

(i) Draw the structural formula for the alkyne formed when the dibromoalkane shown below reacts with sodium hydroxide.

$$H-\underset{\underset{H}{|}}{\overset{\overset{H}{|}}{C}}-\underset{\underset{Br}{|}}{\overset{\overset{H}{|}}{C}}-\underset{\underset{Br}{|}}{\overset{\overset{H}{|}}{C}}-\underset{\underset{H}{|}}{\overset{\overset{H}{|}}{C}}-\underset{\underset{H}{|}}{\overset{\overset{H}{|}}{C}}-H$$

$$\downarrow$$

1

Marks | KU | PS

19. **(b) (continued)**

(ii) Suggest why the dibromoalkane shown below does **not** form an alkyne when heated with sodium hydroxide.

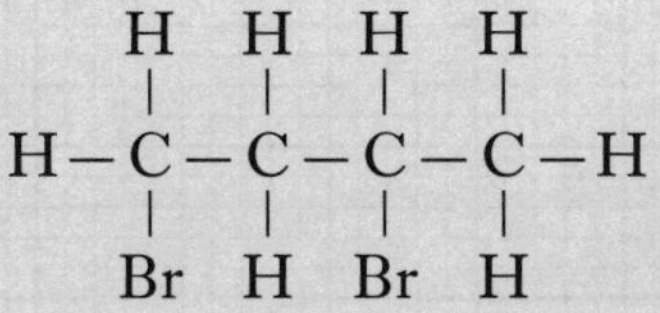

$$
\begin{array}{cccc}
\text{H} & \text{H} & \text{H} & \text{H} \\
| & | & | & | \\
\text{H}-\text{C}-\text{C}-\text{C}-\text{C}-\text{H} \\
| & | & | & | \\
\text{Br} & \text{H} & \text{Br} & \text{H}
\end{array}
$$

_____

_____

_____

1

(3)

[*END OF QUESTION PAPER*]

DO NOT
WRITE IN
THIS
MARGIN

KU PS

ADDITIONAL SPACE FOR ANSWERS

ADDITIONAL GRAPH PAPER FOR QUESTION 12(*d*)(i)

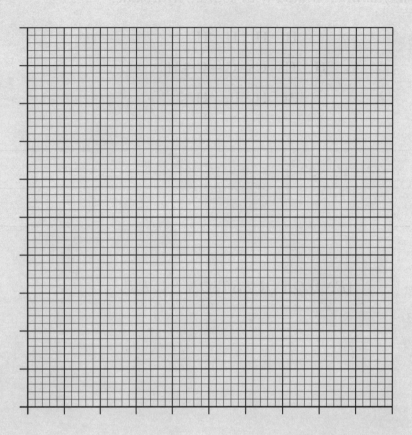

2002 CREDIT

C

FOR OFFICIAL USE

KU   PS

Total Marks

0500/402

NATIONAL
QUALIFICATIONS
2002

THURSDAY, 16 MAY
2.50 PM – 4.20 PM

CHEMISTRY
STANDARD GRADE
Credit Level

Fill in these boxes and read what is printed below.

Full name of centre

Town

Forename(s)

Surname

Date of birth
Day Month Year   Scottish candidate number   Number of seat

1 All questions should be attempted.

2 Necessary data will be found in the Data Booklet provided for Chemistry at Standard Grade and Intermediate 2.

3 The questions may be answered in any order but all answers are to be written in this answer book, and must be written clearly and legibly in ink.

4 Rough work, if any should be necessary, as well as the fair copy, is to be written in this book.

Rough work should be scored through when the fair copy has been written.

5 Additional space for answers and rough work will be found at the end of the book.

6 The size of the space provided for an answer should not be taken as an indication of how much to write. It is not necessary to use all the space.

7 Before leaving the examination room you must give this book to the invigilator. If you do not, you may lose all the marks for this paper.

SCOTTISH
QUALIFICATIONS
AUTHORITY

PART 1

In Questions 1 to 9 of this part of the paper, an answer is given by circling the appropriate letter (or letters) in the answer grid provided.

In some questions, two letters are required for full marks.

If more than the correct number of answers is given, marks will be deducted.

In some cases, the number of correct responses is NOT identified in the question.

A total of 20 marks is available in this part of the paper.

SAMPLE QUESTION

A CH_4	B H_2	C CO_2
D CO	E C_2H_5OH	F C

(a) Identify the hydrocarbon(s).

Ⓐ	B	C
D	E	F

The one correct answer to part (a) is A. This should be circled.

(b) Identify the **two** elements.

A	Ⓑ	C
D	E	Ⓕ

As indicated in this question, there are **two** correct answers to part (b). These are B and F. Both answers are circled.

(c) Identify the substance(s) which can burn to produce **both** carbon dioxide and water.

Ⓐ	B	C
D	Ⓔ	F

There are **two** correct answers to part (c). These are A and E.

Both answers are circled.

If, after you have recorded your answer, you decide that you have made an error and wish to make a change, you should cancel the original answer and circle the answer you now consider to be correct. Thus, in part (a), if you want to change an answer A to an answer D, your answer sheet would look like this:

A̸	B	C
Ⓓ	E	F

If you want to change back to an answer which has already been scored out, you should enter a tick (✓) in the box of the answer of your choice, thus:

✓Ⓐ	B	C
D̸	E	F

Official SQA Past Papers: Credit Chemistry 2002

DO N
WRITE
THIS
MARGIN

KU PS

1. The grid shows the names of some common ionic compounds.

A ammonium chloride	B calcium carbonate	C potassium chloride
D calcium sulphate	E magnesium sulphate	F sodium carbonate

(a) Identify the **two** compounds which could be used as fertilisers.

A	B	C
D	E	F

(b) Identify the **two** compounds which are bases.

A	B	C
D	E	F

[Turn over

2.

Substance	Conducts as		Melting point/°C
	a solid	a liquid	
A	no	yes	801
B	no	no	113
C	yes	yes	63
D	no	no	1700
E	yes	yes	98
F	no	no	44

(a) Identify the substance which could be sodium chloride.

A
B
C
D
E
F

(b) Identify the **two** substances which exist as molecules.

A
B
C
D
E
F

Official SQA Past Papers: Credit Chemistry 2002

DO NOT
WRITE IN
THIS
MARGIN

KU PS

3. The symbols for some elements are shown below.

A	B	C
Li	O	Mg
D	E	F
Si	F	K

(a) Identify the **two** elements which form an ionic compound with a formula of the type XY_2, where X is a metal.

A	B	C
D	E	F

(b) Identify the **two** elements which would react together to form molecules with the same shape as a methane molecule.

A	B	C
D	E	F

[Turn over

4. Hydrocarbons contain hydrogen and carbon only.

(a) Identify the **two** hydrocarbons which would quickly decolourise bromine solution.

A	B	C
D	E	F

(b) Identify the isomer of the hydrocarbon in box D which belongs to a different homologous series.

A	B	C
D	E	F

5.

Particle	Number of		
	protons	neutrons	electrons
A	12	13	12
B	8	10	10
C	12	12	10
D	10	12	10
E	8	10	8

(a) Identify the particle which is a positive ion.

A
B
C
D
E

(b) Identify the **two** particles which are isotopes.

A
B
C
D
E

[Turn over

Page seven

6. An atom of carbon can be represented by the symbol $^{14}_{6}C$.

Identify the correct statement(s) about this carbon atom.

A	It has 14 protons.
B	It has 8 neutrons.
C	It has more protons than neutrons.
D	It has an equal number of protons and neutrons.
E	It has an equal number of protons and electrons.
F	It has an equal number of neutrons and electrons.

A
B
C
D
E
F

Official SQA Past Papers: Credit Chemistry 2002

DO NOT
WRITE IN
THIS
MARGIN

KU | PS

7.

A	B
C_4H_{10} + O_2	$CaCO_3$ + HCl
C	D
Zn + H_2SO_4	Li + H_2O
E	F
CuO + C	Cu + $ZnSO_4$

(a) Which box contains a pair of chemicals that will **not** react with each other?

A	B
C	D
E	F

(b) Which box(es) contain(s) a pair of chemicals that react to form water?

A	B
C	D
E	F

[Turn over

8. Equations are used to represent chemical reactions.

A	$2H_2(g) + O_2(g) \rightarrow 2H_2O(g)$
B	$Zn(s) + FeSO_4(aq) \rightarrow Fe(s) + ZnSO_4(aq)$
C	$Fe^{2+}(aq) \rightarrow Fe^{3+}(aq) + e^-$
D	$CH_4(g) + 2O_2(g) \rightarrow CO_2(g) + 2H_2O(g)$
E	$2H_2O(\ell) + O_2(g) + 4e^- \rightarrow 4OH^-(aq)$
F	$Fe^{2+}(aq) + 2e^- \rightarrow Fe(s)$

(a) Identify the **two** equations which represent combustion reactions.

A
B
C
D
E
F

(b) Identify the equation(s) which represent(s) a step in the rusting of iron.

A
B
C
D
E
F

9. Identify the statement(s) which refer(s) to an atom of fluorine.

You may wish to use the data booklet to help you.

A	It has a stable electron arrangement.
B	It will form an ion by losing one electron.
C	It will form an ion with a single negative charge.
D	It has two more electrons than an oxygen atom.
E	It has the same number of electrons as a chlorine atom.
F	It has the same number of outer electrons as an iodine atom.

A
B
C
D
E
F

[Turn over

Marks | KU | PS

PART 2

A total of 40 marks is available in this part of the paper.

10. Ethene is a starting material in the manufacture of the polymer poly(vinylchloride), PVC.

(a) Name the process used to make ethene from hydrocarbons obtained from crude oil.

_____

1

(b) Part of a PVC molecule is shown below.

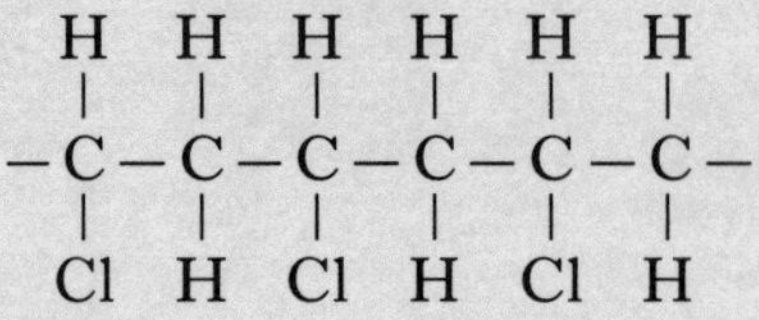

$$\begin{array}{cccccc} H & H & H & H & H & H \\ | & | & | & | & | & | \\ -C-&C-&C-&C-&C-&C- \\ | & | & | & | & | & | \\ Cl & H & Cl & H & Cl & H \end{array}$$

(i) Draw the structure of the repeating unit in a PVC molecule.

1

(ii) Name a toxic gas produced when PVC burns.

_____

1

(3)

Marks | KU | PS

11. (*a*) Ailsa carried out the experiment shown below.

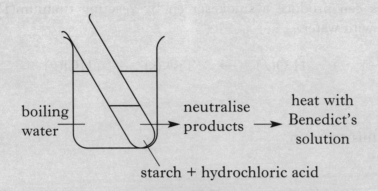

boiling
water

starch + hydrochloric acid

neutralise
products

heat with
Benedict's
solution

**Result:
Benedict's solution
turns red/orange**

(i) What type of chemical reaction takes place when starch is heated with hydrochloric acid?

_____ 1

(ii) Ailsa said that the starch had turned into glucose.

Name another sugar which turns Benedict's solution red/orange.

_____ 1

(iii) Ailsa repeated her experiment using amylase solution instead of hydrochloric acid.

Suggest a reason why the Benedict's solution did not turn red/orange.

_____ 1

(*b*) Write the molecular formula for glucose.

_____ 1

(4)

[Turn over

Marks | KU | PS

12. Titanium compounds have many uses.

(a) (i) Warships can produce a smokescreen by reacting titanium(IV) chloride with water:

$$TiCl_4(\ell) \quad + \quad H_2O(\ell) \quad \rightarrow \quad TiO_2(s) \quad + \quad HCl(g)$$

Balance this equation.

1

(ii) Titanium(IV) chloride is a liquid at room temperature.

What type of bonding does this suggest is present in titanium(IV) chloride?

_____

1

(b) Titanium(IV) oxide (TiO_2) is used as a white pigment in paint.

Calculate the percentage by mass of titanium in TiO_2.

(Relative atomic mass of titanium = 48)

Show your working clearly.

2

(4)

13. Copper displaces silver from silver(I) nitrate solution.

$$Cu(s) + 2Ag^+(aq) + 2NO_3^-(aq) \rightarrow Cu^{2+}(aq) + 2NO_3^-(aq) + 2Ag(s)$$

(*a*) Rewrite the equation omitting the spectator ions.

1

(*b*) Write the ion-electron equation for the oxidation step in the displacement reaction.

You may wish to use the data booklet to help you.

1

(*c*) The reaction can also be carried out in a cell.

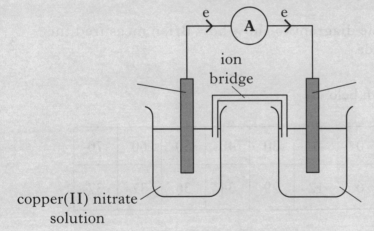

copper(II) nitrate
solution

(i) Complete the three labels on the diagram.

1

(ii) The purpose of the ion bridge is to complete the circuit.

Suggest why sodium carbonate solution should not be used in the ion bridge.

You may wish to use the data booklet to help you.

_____

_____

_____

1

(4)

[Turn over

Marks | KU | PS

14. Sodium carbonate reacts with hydrochloric acid to form carbon dioxide. Brian measured the volume of carbon dioxide given off over a period of time and recorded his results.

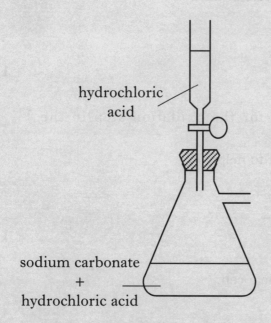

hydrochloric acid

sodium carbonate
+
hydrochloric acid

(a) Complete and label the diagram to show how Brian measured the volume of carbon dioxide.

2

(b) Brian's results are shown below.

Time/s	0	10	30	40	50	60	70
Volume of carbon dioxide/cm^3	0	12	29	34	36	37	37

Marks | KU | PS

14. **(b)** **(continued)**

Draw a line graph of the results.

Use appropriate scales to fill most of the graph paper.

(Additional graph paper, if required, will be found on page 26.)

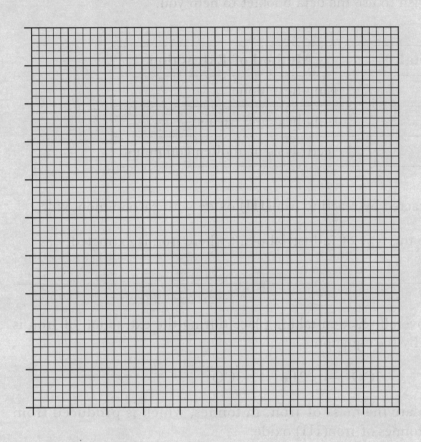

2

(c) Suggest a value for the volume of carbon dioxide collected during the first 20 seconds.

_____ cm^3

1

(d) Write the ionic formula for sodium carbonate.

_____

1

(6)

[Turn over

Marks KU PS

15. Some metals are found uncombined in the Earth's crust but others have to be extracted from their ores.

(a) Place the following metals in the correct space in the table.

lead, magnesium, mercury

You may wish to use the data booklet to help you.

Metal	Method of Extraction
	using heat alone
	using heat and carbon
	electrolysis of molten compound

1

(b) Iron is extracted by reacting iron(III) oxide with carbon monoxide.

(i) Name the type of industrial plant where iron is extracted.

_____

1

(ii) The overall reaction taking place during the extraction of iron is given by the equation:

$$Fe_2O_3 \ + \ 3CO \ \rightarrow \ 2Fe \ + \ 3CO_2$$

Calculate the mass of iron, in tonnes, which is produced from 1600 tonnes of iron(III) oxide.

Show your working clearly.

Answer: _____ tonnes

2

(4)

Marks | KU | PS

16. Fermentation is used to produce alcohol from sugars like glucose.

(a) Name the gas produced during the fermentation of glucose.

_____

1

(b) Why does fermentation stop when the alcohol concentration reaches approximately 15 %?

_____

_____

1

(c) In industry, ethanol (alcohol) can be produced from ethene as shown below.

$$H-\overset{\displaystyle H}{\underset{\displaystyle H}{C}}=\overset{\displaystyle H}{\underset{\displaystyle H}{C}}-H \quad + \quad H_2O \quad \longrightarrow \quad H-\overset{\displaystyle H}{\underset{\displaystyle H}{C}}-\overset{\displaystyle OH}{\underset{\displaystyle H}{C}}-H$$

ethene   ethanol

  (i) Name the type of chemical reaction taking place.

_____

1

  (ii) Draw a structural formula for the product of the following reaction:

$$H-\overset{\displaystyle H}{\underset{\displaystyle H}{C}}=\overset{\displaystyle H}{\underset{\displaystyle CH_3}{C}}-\overset{\displaystyle H}{\underset{\displaystyle H}{C}}-\overset{\displaystyle H}{\underset{\displaystyle H}{C}}-H \quad + \quad H_2O$$

$$\downarrow$$

1

(4)

[Turn over

Marks | KU | PS

17. Alcohols can be oxidised by hot copper(II) oxide.

The product is either an aldehyde or a ketone.

Alcohol	Structural formula	Type of product	Structural formula
ethanol	H and H atoms on two carbons: H–C–C–OH with H above and below each C	an aldehyde	H–C–C=O structure with H atoms and double-bonded O, terminal H
propan-1-ol	H–C–C–C–OH with H atoms above and below each C	an aldehyde	H–C–C–C=O with H atoms and terminal H
propan-2-ol	H–C–C–C–H with H, OH, H below	a ketone	H–C–C–C–H with H, O (double bond), H
butan-2-ol	H–C–C–C–C–H with H, OH, H, H below	a ketone	H–C–C–C–C–H with H, O (double bond), H, H

(a) (i) Aldehydes and ketones have the same general formula.

Suggest a general formula for these compounds.

_____ 1

(ii) Write a general statement linking the type of product to the structure of the alcohol used.

_____

_____

_____ 1

Marks | KU | PS

17. (continued)

(*b*) In these reactions the copper(II) oxide is reduced to copper metal.
Suggest why aluminium oxide cannot be used to oxidise alcohols.

_____

_____

_____

1

(3)

[Turn over

DO NOT
WRITE IN
THIS
MARGIN

Marks | KU | PS

18. The flow chart shows some processes which take place in an industrial chemical complex.

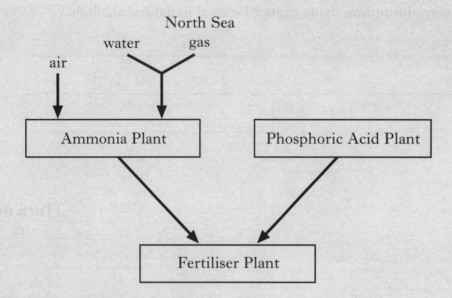

(a) Air and water are used as raw materials because they contain the elements needed to make ammonia.

Suggest **one** other reason why they are used as raw materials.

_____

_____ 1

(b) Which reactant for the ammonia plant must be produced in the reaction between North Sea gas and water?

_____ 1

(c) Name the salt formed in the fertiliser plant.

_____ 1

Marks | KU | PS

18. (continued)

(*d*) The graph shows the different percentage yields of ammonia which can be obtained under different conditions in the ammonia plant.

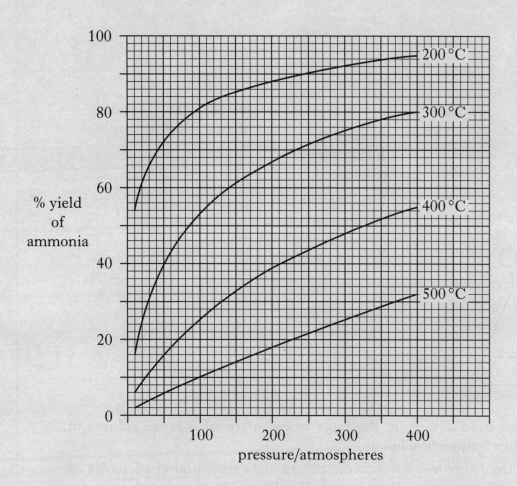

(i) What is the relationship between the percentage yield of ammonia and the temperature at constant pressure?

_____

_____

_____   1

(ii) Explain why all of the nitrogen and hydrogen are not converted to ammonia.

_____

_____

_____   1

(5)

[Turn over

Marks | KU | PS

19. Vinegar is a dilute solution of ethanoic acid in water.

Karen carried out a titration to find out the concentration of ethanoic acid in some vinegar.

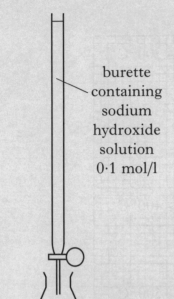

burette containing sodium hydroxide solution 0·1 mol/l

	Rough titre	1st titre	2nd titre
Initial burette reading/cm^3	1·0	21·7	11·7
Final burette reading/cm^3	21·7	41·7	31·9
Volume used/cm^3	20·7	20·0	20·2

25 cm^3 vinegar plus indicator

(a) Karen used data from the table to calculate an average volume of sodium hydroxide solution.

She used this average volume to calculate the number of moles of sodium hydroxide needed to neutralise the acid in 25 cm^3 of the vinegar.

(i) What average volume of sodium hydroxide should she have used?

_____ cm^3

1

19. (*a*) **(continued)**

Marks | KU | PS

(ii) Calculate the number of moles of sodium hydroxide in this average volume.

Show your working clearly.

1

(*b*) 1 mole of ethanoic acid reacts with 1 mole of sodium hydroxide.

Calculate the concentration, in mol/l, of ethanoic acid in the vinegar.

Show your working clearly

1

(3)

[END OF QUESTION PAPER]

Official SQA Past Papers: Credit Chemistry 2002

DO NOT
WRITE IN
THIS
MARGIN

KU | PS

ADDITIONAL SPACE FOR ANSWERS

ADDITIONAL GRAPH PAPER FOR QUESTION 14(*b*)

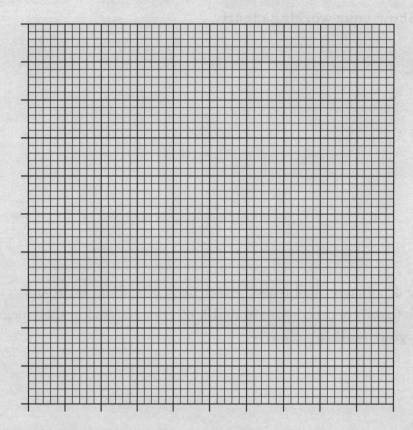

ADDITIONAL SPACE FOR ANSWERS

ADDITIONAL SPACE FOR ANSWERS

2003 CREDIT

FOR OFFICIAL USE

C

KU   PS

Total Marks

0500/402

NATIONAL
QUALIFICATIONS
2003

FRIDAY, 23 MAY
10.50 AM – 12.20 PM

CHEMISTRY
STANDARD GRADE
Credit Level

Fill in these boxes and read what is printed below.

Full name of centre

Town

Forename(s)

Surname

Date of birth
Day Month Year   Scottish candidate number   Number of seat

1 All questions should be attempted.

2 Necessary data will be found in the Data Booklet provided for Chemistry at Standard Grade and Intermediate 2.

3 The questions may be answered in any order but all answers are to be written in this answer book, and must be written clearly and legibly in ink.

4 Rough work, if any should be necessary, as well as the fair copy, is to be written in this book.

Rough work should be scored through when the fair copy has been written.

5 Additional space for answers and rough work will be found at the end of the book.

6 The size of the space provided for an answer should not be taken as an indication of how much to write. It is not necessary to use all the space.

7 Before leaving the examination room you must give this book to the invigilator. If you do not, you may lose all the marks for this paper.

SCOTTISH
QUALIFICATIONS
AUTHORITY

©

PART 1

In Questions 1 to 9 of this part of the paper, an answer is given by circling the appropriate letter (or letters) in the answer grid provided.

In some questions, two letters are required for full marks.

If more than the correct number of answers is given, marks will be deducted.

In some cases, the number of correct responses is NOT identified in the question.

A total of 20 marks is available in this part of the paper.

SAMPLE QUESTION

A CH_4	B H_2	C CO_2
D CO	E C_2H_5OH	F C

(a) Identify the hydrocarbon(s).

Ⓐ	B	C
D	E	F

The one correct answer to part (a) is A. This should be circled.

(b) Identify the **two** elements.

A	Ⓑ	C
D	E	Ⓕ

As indicated in this question, there are **two** correct answers to part (b). These are B and F. Both answers are circled.

(c) Identify the substance(s) which can burn to produce **both** carbon dioxide and water.

Ⓐ	B	C
D	Ⓔ	F

There are **two** correct answers to part (c). These are A and E.

Both answers are circled.

If, after you have recorded your answer, you decide that you have made an error and wish to make a change, you should cancel the original answer and circle the answer you now consider to be correct. Thus, in part (a), if you want to change an answer A to an answer D, your answer sheet would look like this:

Ⓐ̸	B	C
Ⓓ	E	F

If you want to change back to an answer which has already been scored out, you should enter a tick (✓) in the box of the answer of your choice, thus:

✓Ⓐ̸	B	C
Ⓓ̸	E	F

1. Atoms are made up of protons, neutrons and electrons.

A	The number of protons
B	The number of neutrons
C	The number of electrons
D	The number of outer electrons
E	The number of protons plus neutrons

(a) Identify the **two** numbers which are the same in a neutral atom.

A
B
C
D
E

(b) Identify the mass number of an atom.

A
B
C
D
E

[Turn over

Official SQA Past Papers: Credit Chemistry 2003

DO NOT
WRITE IN
THIS
MARGIN

KU PS

2. The names of several compounds are shown in the grid.

A potassium nitrate	B sodium hydroxide	C lithium sulphate
D aluminium chloride	E ammonium phosphate	F calcium chloride

(a) Identify the **two** compounds which can be used as fertilisers.

A	B	C
D	E	F

(b) Identify the **two** compounds which react together to produce ammonia.

A	B	C
D	E	F

3. Hydrocarbons are compounds made from hydrogen and carbon only.

A	B	C
$\begin{array}{c} H \\ \diagdown \\ H \diagup \end{array} C = C \begin{array}{c} H \\ \diagup \\ \diagdown H \end{array}$	$\begin{array}{ccccccc} & H & H & H & H & \\ & \mid & \mid & \mid & \mid & \\ H- & C- & C- & C- & C & -H \\ & \mid & \mid & \mid & \mid & \\ & H & H & H & H & \end{array}$	$\begin{array}{c} H \quad H \\ \diagdown \diagup \\ C \\ \diagup \diagdown \\ H-C - C-H \\ \diagup \qquad \diagdown \\ H \qquad\quad H \end{array}$

D	E	F
$\begin{array}{c} \quad\quad H \\ H \quad\quad \mid \\ \diagdown \quad\quad \mid \\ C=C-C-H \\ \diagup \quad \mid \;\; \mid \\ H \quad H \;\; H \end{array}$	$\begin{array}{c} H \quad H \\ \diagdown \diagup \\ H \quad C \quad H \\ \diagdown \mid \diagup \\ H-C \quad C-H \\ \mid \quad\;\; \mid \\ H-C - C-H \\ \mid \quad\;\; \mid \\ H \quad H \end{array}$	$\begin{array}{c} \quad\quad H \;\; H \\ H \quad \mid \;\; \mid \\ \diagdown \quad \mid \;\; \mid \\ C=C-C-C-H \\ \diagup \quad \mid \;\; \mid \;\; \mid \\ H \quad H \;\; H \;\; H \end{array}$

(a) Identify the hydrocarbon which reacts with hydrogen to form butane.

A	B	C
D	E	F

(b) Identify the **two** isomers.

A	B	C
D	E	F

(c) Identify the hydrocarbon(s) which is (are) the first member(s) of a homologous series.

A	B	C
D	E	F

[Turn over

4. The grid shows some pairs of chemicals.

A sodium + water	B zinc + magnesium sulphate solution
C copper carbonate + dilute sulphuric acid	D lead nitrate solution + potassium iodide solution
E silver + dilute hydrochloric acid	F potassium hydroxide solution + dilute nitric acid

Which box(es) contain(s) a pair of chemicals that react to form a gas?

A	B
C	D
E	F

Page six

5. Identify the result(s) obtained in the reaction between dilute sulphuric acid and barium hydroxide solution.

You may wish to use the data booklet to help you.

A	The pH of the acid went down.
B	Carbon dioxide was produced.
C	A precipitate was formed.
D	Hydrogen was produced.
E	Water was produced.

A
B
C
D
E

[Turn over

6. Oil rigs made from iron should be protected from rusting.

Identify the correct statement(s).

A	Salt water slows down rusting.
B	Tin gives sacrificial protection to the iron.
C	The rusting of iron is an example of oxidation.
D	Ferroxyl indicator turns blue in the presence of Fe^{2+} ions.
E	Iron rusts faster when connected to the negative terminal of a battery.

A
B
C
D
E

7. Iron(III) oxide is an ionic compound.

Identify the correct statement(s).

A	It is a salt.
B	It can be reduced to iron.
C	It has the formula Fe_2O_3.
D	It is made up of molecules.
E	It does not react with acid.

| A |
| B |
| C |
| D |
| E |

[Turn over

8. The table contains information about some solid, liquid and gaseous compounds.

Compound	Melting point /°C	Boiling point /°C	pH of solution in water
A	319	1390	11
B	801	1413	7
C	−115	−85	3
D	−93	−6	11
E	−95	56	7
F	63	189	3

(a) Identify the compound which is a gas at 25 °C and forms an acidic solution.

A
B
C
D
E
F

(b) Identify the compound which could be sodium hydroxide.

A
B
C
D
E
F

9. Substances can be classified as conductors or non-conductors and also as solids or liquids.

Substance	State	Conductor or non-conductor
A	solid	non-conductor
B	liquid	non-conductor
C	solid	conductor
D	liquid	conductor

(a) Which **two** substances could be sodium chloride?

A
B
C
D

(b) Which substance could **not** be a compound?

A
B
C
D

[Turn over

Marks | KU | PS

PART 2

A total of 40 marks is available in this part of the paper.

10.   The diagrams show how different flames can be produced in a Bunsen burner.

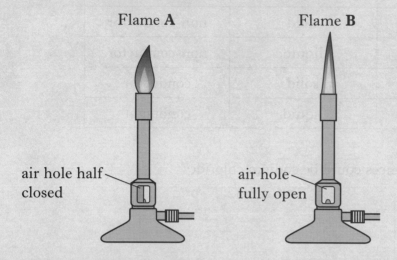

Flame **A**   Flame **B**

air hole half
closed

air hole
fully open

(a)   The fuel used in a Bunsen burner is methane, CH_4.
What is meant by the term "fuel"?

_____

_____   1

(b)   Methane burns to form carbon dioxide and water.

(i)   Balance this equation.

$$CH_4 \quad + \quad O_2 \quad \rightarrow \quad CO_2 \quad + \quad H_2O$$

1

(ii)   Name another product which could be formed in Flame **A**.

_____   1

(c)   Draw a diagram to show the **shape** of a methane molecule.

1

(4)

Marks | KU | PS

11. There are two different types of chlorine atom: $^{35}_{17}Cl$ and $^{37}_{17}Cl$.

(a) (i) What name is used to describe these different types of chlorine atom?

_____   1

(ii) A natural sample of chlorine has an average atomic mass of 35·5.
What is the mass number of the more abundant type of chlorine atom in the sample?

_____   1

(b) The atoms in a chlorine molecule are held together by a covalent bond. A covalent bond is a shared pair of electrons.
Explain how this holds the atoms together.

_____

_____

_____

_____

_____   1

(c) Complete the table to show the number of each type of particle in a $^{35}_{17}Cl^-$ ion.

Particle	Number
proton	
neutron	
electron	

2

(5)

[Turn over

Marks | KU | PS

12. Hydrogen can be produced in the laboratory by adding excess hydrochloric acid to lumps of zinc. The reaction stops when all the zinc is used up.

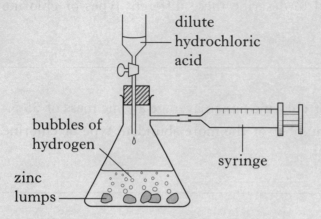

dilute
hydrochloric
acid

bubbles of
hydrogen

zinc
lumps

syringe

The volume of hydrogen gas produced over a period of time was measured and the results are shown in the table.

Time/s	0	20	40	60	80	100	120	140
Volume of hydrogen/cm^3	0	30	51	65	74	78	80	80

(a) Draw a line graph of the results.

Use appropriate scales to fill most of the graph paper.

(Additional graph paper, if required, will be found on page 24.)

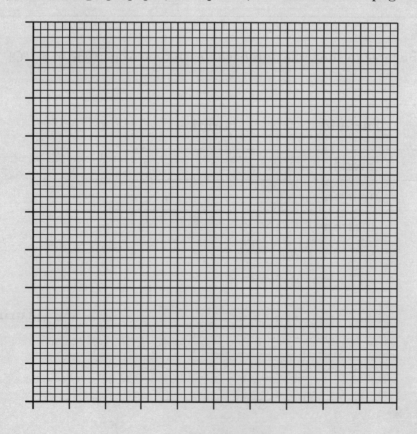

2

Marks | KU | PS

12. **(continued)**

(*b*) Use your graph to estimate the time, in seconds, for $40 \, cm^3$ of hydrogen to be produced.

_____ 1

(*c*) The equation for the reaction of zinc with hydrochloric acid is

$$Zn \quad + \quad 2HCl \quad \rightarrow \quad ZnCl_2 \quad + \quad H_2$$

Calculate the mass of zinc required to produce 0·5 mole of hydrogen.

Answer: _____ g   1

(4)

[Turn over

Marks | KU | PS

13. Mrs Smith gave her class three chemicals labelled **P**, **Q** and **R**.

The chemicals were ethanol (C_2H_5OH) solution, silver nitrate solution and dilute sulphuric acid.

The class used the following apparatus to identify each solution.

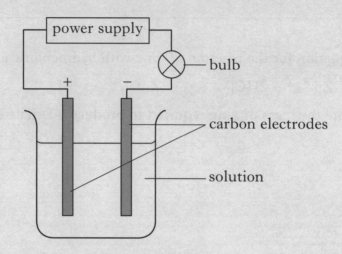

The results are shown in the table.

Solution	Bulb lights	Observation at electrodes
P	Yes	grey solid formed at negative electrode
Q	No	no reaction
R	Yes	a gas formed at both electrodes

(a) Identify **P**.

_____ 1

(b) What type of bonding is present in **Q**?

_____ 1

(c) Name the gas formed at the negative electrode when solution **R** is used.

_____ 1

(d) What process would be used to obtain a sample of ethanol from the ethanol solution?

_____ 1

(4)

Marks | KU | PS

14. Propene has the structural formula shown below.

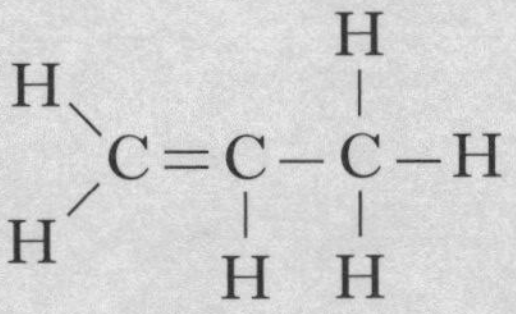

$$\begin{array}{c} \quad\quad\quad\quad H \\ \quad\quad\quad\quad | \\ \overset{H}{\underset{H}{>}}C=\underset{|}{\overset{|}{C}}-\underset{|}{\overset{|}{C}}-H \\ \quad\quad\quad H\;\;H \end{array}$$

Propene quickly decolourises bromine water, $Br_2(aq)$.

(*a*) (i) Name the type of chemical reaction which takes place when propene reacts with bromine water.

_____ 1

(ii) Draw the **full** structural formula for the product of the reaction.

1

(*b*) Propene can be converted into the polymer, poly(propene).

Complete the diagram to show how **three** propene molecules join to form part of the polymer chain.

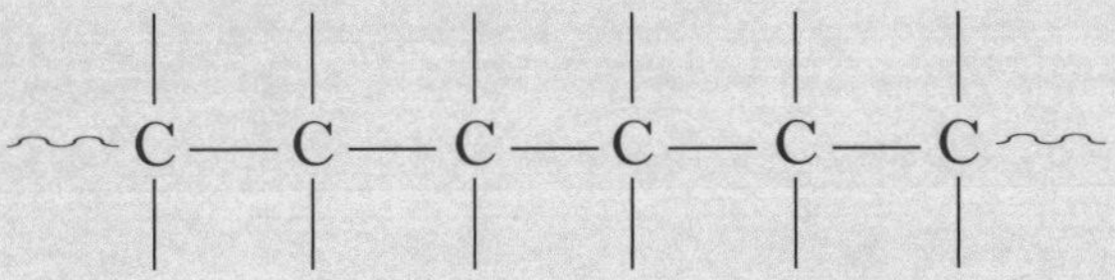

$$\sim\!\!\sim C - C - C - C - C - C \!\!\sim\!\!\sim$$

1

(3)

[Turn over

DO NOT
WRITE IN
THIS
MARGIN

Marks | KU | PS

15. Bones are formed when calcium ions and phosphate ions combine to form insoluble calcium phosphate, $Ca_3(PO_4)_2$.

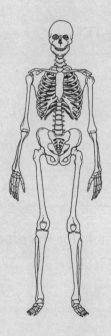

This reaction can be reproduced in the laboratory by adding a solution of calcium chloride to a solution of sodium phosphate.

$$3Ca^{2+}(aq) + 6Cl^-(aq) + 6Na^+(aq) + 2PO_4^{3-}(aq) \rightarrow 6Na^+(aq) + 6Cl^-(aq) + (Ca^{2+})_3(PO_4^{3-})_2(s)$$

(*a*) Circle the spectator ions in the above equation.   **1**

(*b*) What technique could be used to remove the calcium phosphate from the mixture?

_____   **1**

(*c*) Calculate the percentage by mass of calcium in calcium phosphate, $Ca_3(PO_4)_2$.

Answer: _____ %   **2**

(4)

Marks | KU | PS

16. Helen set up the cell shown below.

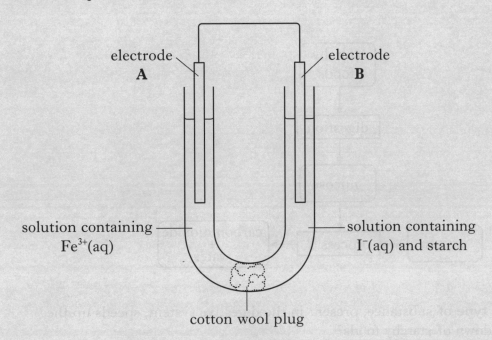

electrode **A**

electrode **B**

solution containing $Fe^{3+}(aq)$

solution containing $I^-(aq)$ and starch

cotton wool plug

The reaction taking place at electrode **A** is

$$Fe^{3+}(aq) \ + \ e^- \ \rightarrow \ Fe^{2+}(aq)$$

(*a*) (i) **On the diagram**, clearly mark the path and the direction of electron flow.

_____ 1

(ii) What term is used to describe the type of chemical reaction taking place at electrode **A**?

_____ 1

(*b*) Iodine forms at electrode **B**.

(i) What would you **see** happening around electrode **B**?

_____

_____ 1

(ii) Write an ion-electron equation for the chemical reaction taking place at electrode **B**.

You may wish to use the data booklet to help you.

_____ 1

(4)

[Turn over

Marks | KU | PS

17. The flow diagram shows what happens to starchy foods after they have been eaten.

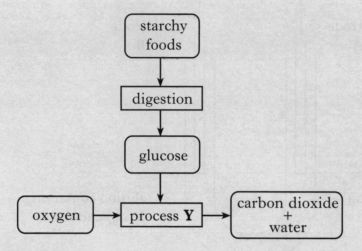

(a) What **type** of substance, present in the digestive system, speeds up the breakdown of starchy foods?

_____   **1**

(b) What **type** of chemical reaction takes place when starch is broken down into glucose during digestion?

_____   **1**

(c) Process **Y** provides the body with energy.
Name this process.

_____   **1**

(d) Name an isomer of glucose.

_____   **1**

(4)

Marks KU PS

18. The energy required to remove an outer electron from an atom is called the ionisation energy.

(a) The equation for the ionisation of a magnesium atom is

$$Mg(g) \longrightarrow Mg^+(g) + e^-$$

Write the electron arrangement for $Mg^+(g)$.

_____ 1

(b) The graph shows the ionisation energy values for the first 20 elements.

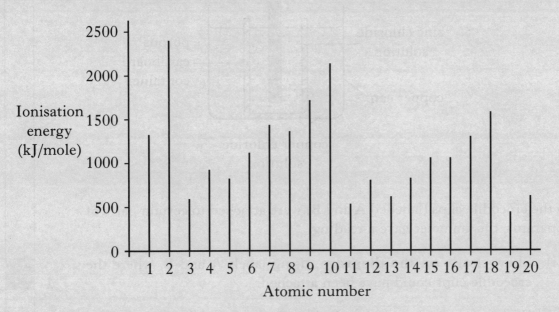

(i) Describe the general trend in ionisation energy going from lithium to neon.

_____

_____

_____ 1

(ii) Describe the trend in ionisation energy going down a group.

_____

_____

_____ 1

(3)

[Turn over

Marks | KU | PS

19. Roy wanted to show that chemicals can be used to produce an electric current.

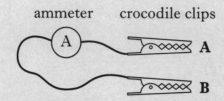

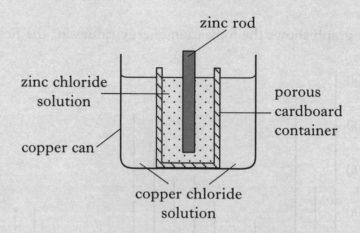

When the crocodile clips (labelled **A** and **B**) were attached to certain parts of the apparatus, the ammeter gave a reading.

(a) (i) Show clearly **on the diagram**, using labels **A** and **B**, where the crocodile clips could have been attached. 1

(ii) Why was no current produced when the porous cardboard container was replaced by a glass beaker?

_____

_____

_____ 1

(iii) What would happen to the reading on the ammeter if the zinc rod was replaced with a tin rod in a tin chloride solution?

_____ 1

DO NOT WRITE IN THIS MARGIN

Marks | KU | PS

19. (continued)

(*b*) Roy was instructed to make 50 cm^3 of a 1 mol/litre solution of copper chloride, $CuCl_2$.

Calculate the mass, in grams, of copper chloride needed.

Show your working clearly

Answer: ________________ g **2**

(5)

[*END OF QUESTION PAPER*]

DO NOT
WRITE IN
THIS
MARGIN

KU | PS

ADDITIONAL SPACE FOR ANSWERS

ADDITIONAL GRAPH PAPER FOR QUESTION 12(*a*)

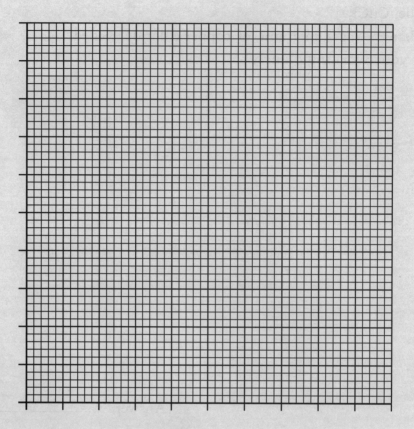

C

FOR OFFICIAL USE

	KU	PS
Total Marks		

0500/402

NATIONAL
QUALIFICATIONS
2004

MONDAY, 10 MAY
10.50 AM – 12.20 PM

**CHEMISTRY
STANDARD GRADE**
Credit Level

Fill in these boxes and read what is printed below.

Full name of centre

Town

Forename(s)

Surname

Date of birth

Day   Month   Year   Scottish candidate number   Number of seat

1 All questions should be attempted.

2 Necessary data will be found in the Data Booklet provided for Chemistry at Standard Grade and Intermediate 2.

3 The questions may be answered in any order but all answers are to be written in this answer book, and must be written clearly and legibly in ink.

4 Rough work, if any should be necessary, as well as the fair copy, is to be written in this book.
Rough work should be scored through when the fair copy has been written.

5 Additional space for answers and rough work will be found at the end of the book.

6 The size of the space provided for an answer should not be taken as an indication of how much to write. It is not necessary to use all the space.

7 Before leaving the examination room you must give this book to the invigilator. If you do not, you may lose all the marks for this paper.

**SCOTTISH
QUALIFICATIONS
AUTHORITY**

PART 1

In Questions 1 to 9 of this part of the paper, an answer is given by circling the appropriate letter (or letters) in the answer grid provided.

In some questions, two letters are required for full marks.

If more than the correct number of answers is given, marks will be deducted.

A total of 20 marks is available in this part of the paper.

SAMPLE QUESTION

A CH_4	B H_2	C CO_2
D CO	E C_2H_5OH	F C

(a) Identify the hydrocarbon.

Ⓐ	B	C
D	E	F

The correct answer to part (a) is A. This should be circled.

(b) Identify the **two** elements.

A	Ⓑ	C
D	E	Ⓕ

As indicated in this question, there are **two** correct answers to part (b). These are B and F. Both answers are circled.

If, after you have recorded your answer, you decide that you have made an error and wish to make a change, you should cancel the original answer and circle the answer you now consider to be correct. Thus, in part (a), if you want to change an answer A to an answer D, your answer sheet would look like this:

Ⓐ̶	B	C
Ⓓ	E	F

If you want to change back to an answer which has already been scored out, you should enter a tick (✓) in the box of the answer of your choice, thus:

✓Ⓐ̶	B	C
Ⓓ̶	E	F

DO NOT WRITE IN THIS MARGIN

Marks KU PS

1. The grid shows the formulae of six oxides.

A	B	C
H_2O	NO_2	K_2O
D	E	F
CaO	CO	SO_2

(*a*) Identify the oxide produced by the sparking of air in car engines.

A	B	C
D	E	F

1

(*b*) Identify the **two** oxides produced by burning hydrocarbons.

A	B	C
D	E	F

1

(2)

[Turn over

DO NOT WRITE IN THIS MARGIN

Marks | KU | PS

2. The names of some hydrocarbons are shown in the grid.

A cyclobutane	B cyclopentane	C butane
D propane	E ethane	F butene

(*a*) Identify the hydrocarbon which is a liquid at 25 °C.

You may wish to use the data booklet to help you.

A	B	C
D	E	F

1

(*b*) Identify the **two** isomers.

A	B	C
D	E	F

1

(*c*) Identify the hydrocarbon that reacts quickly with bromine solution.

A	B	C
D	E	F

1

(3)

Marks KU PS

3. The grid shows the names of some soluble compounds.

A	B	C
magnesium bromide	sodium bromide	lithium hydroxide
D	E	F
sodium iodide	potassium sulphate	lithium chloride

(*a*) Identify the base.

A	B	C
D	E	F

1

(*b*) Identify the **two** compounds whose solutions would form a precipitate when mixed.

You may wish to use the data booklet to help you.

A	B	C
D	E	F

1

(*c*) Identify the compound with a formula of the type **XY$_2$**, where **X** is a metal.

A	B	C
D	E	F

1

(3)

[Turn over

Official SQA Past Papers: Credit Chemistry 2004

DO NOT
WRITE IN
THIS
MARGIN

Marks | KU | PS

4. A pupil carried out the following experiments.

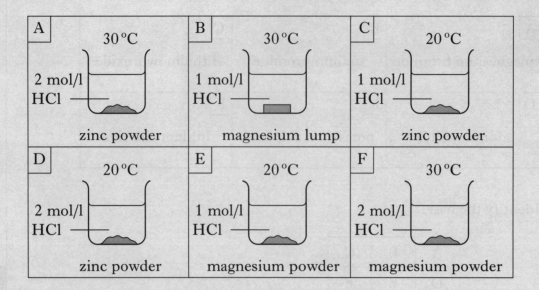

(a) Identify the **two** experiments which can be used to investigate the effect of concentration on the rate of the reaction.

A	B	C
D	E	F

1

(b) Identify the experiment with the fastest reaction rate.

A	B	C
D	E	F

1
(2)

Marks | KU | PS

5. The table contains information about some substances.

Substance	Melting point/°C	Boiling point/°C	Conducts as	
			a solid	a liquid
A	455	1567	no	yes
B	80	218	no	no
C	1492	2897	yes	yes
D	1407	2357	no	no
E	645	1287	no	yes
F	98	890	yes	yes

(a) Identify the **two** ionic compounds.

A
B
C
D
E
F

1

(b) Identify the substance which exists as a covalent network.

A
B
C
D
E
F

1

(2)

[Turn over

Marks | KU | PS

6. The grid shows information about some particles.

A	B	C
$^{34}_{16}S^{2-}$	$^{24}_{12}Mg^{2+}$	$^{39}_{19}K$

D	E	F
$^{40}_{19}K$	$^{40}_{20}Ca$	$^{35}_{17}Cl^-$

(a) Identify the **two** particles which are isotopes.

A	B	C
D	E	F

1

(b) Identify the **two** particles with the same electron arrangement as argon.

A	B	C
D	E	F

1

(2)

Marks | KU | PS

7. The grid contains information about the particles found in atoms.

A	B	C
charge = zero	relative mass almost zero	charge = 1–
D	E	F
found inside the nucleus	charge = 1+	relative mass = 1

Identify the **two** terms which can be applied to electrons.

A	B	C
D	E	F

(2)

[Turn over

8. Glucose, sucrose and starch are carbohydrates.

Identify the **two** correct statements.

A	Glucose molecules join together with the loss of water.
B	Starch is a polymer made from sucrose molecules.
C	Sucrose turns warm Benedict's solution orange.
D	Glucose is an isomer of sucrose.
E	Starch dissolves easily in water.
F	Sucrose can be hydrolysed.

A
B
C
D
E
F

(2)

Marks KU | PS

9. The diagram shows how an object can be coated in nickel.

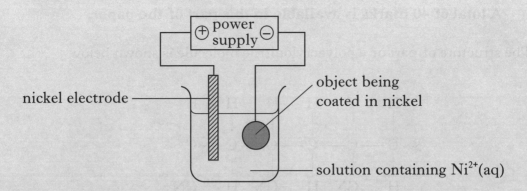

The following reactions take place at the electrodes.

Negative electrode: $Ni^{2+}(aq) + 2e^- \rightarrow Ni(s)$

Positive electrode: $Ni(s) \rightarrow Ni^{2+}(aq) + 2e^-$

Identify the **two** correct statements.

A	Nickel ions move towards the nickel electrode.
B	The mass of the nickel electrode decreases.
C	The process is an example of galvanising.
D	Oxidation occurs at the nickel electrode.
E	Electrons flow through the solution.

A
B
C
D
E

(2)

[Turn over

DO NOT WRITE IN THIS MARGIN

Marks | KU | PS

PART 2

A total of 40 marks is available in this part of the paper.

10. The structure of part of a polyacrylonitrile molecule is shown below.

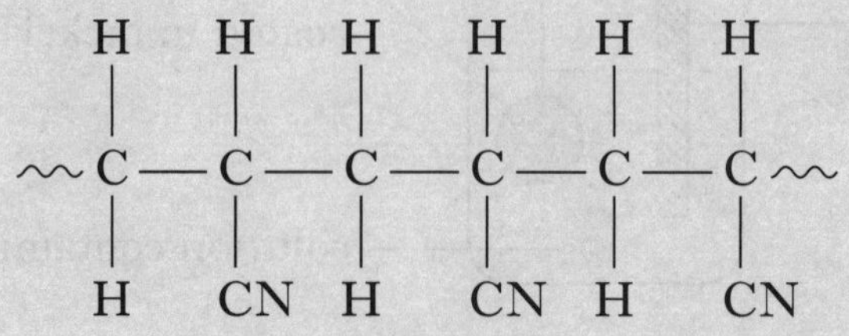
H H H H H H
C — C — C — C — C — C
H CN H CN H CN

(*a*) Draw the structural formula for the monomer used to make polyacrylonitrile. **1**

(*b*) Name a toxic gas produced when polyacrylonitrile burns.

____ **1**

(2)

11. Some Euro coins are made from a hard-wearing alloy called Nordic Gold.

(a) What is an alloy?

_____

_____   1

(b) The composition of Nordic Gold is shown in the table.

Metal	copper	aluminium	zinc	tin
% by mass	89	5	5	1

One of the coins has a mass of 5·74 g.

(i) Calculate the mass, in grams, of aluminium in the coin.
Show your working clearly.

_____ g   1

(ii) Calculate the number of moles of aluminium in the coin.
Show your working clearly.

_____ mol   1

(3)

[Turn over

Marks | KU | PS

12. A group of pupils investigated the speed of reaction between marble chips (calcium carbonate) and hydrochloric acid, concentration 1 mol/l.

They used excess hydrochloric acid to make sure all the calcium carbonate had been used up.

The pupils used a balance to measure the mass lost during the reaction.

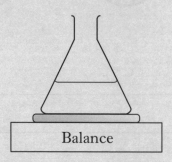

Balance

The results are shown in the table.

Time/minutes	0	0·5	1·0	2·0	3·0	4·0	5·0
Mass lost/g	0	0·30	0·50	0·70	0·76	0·79	0·80

(a) Why is mass lost during the reaction?

_____

_____   1

Marks | KU | PS

12. (continued)

(*b*) Draw a line graph of the results.

Use appropriate scales to fill most of the graph paper.

(Additional graph paper, if required, will be found on page 26.)

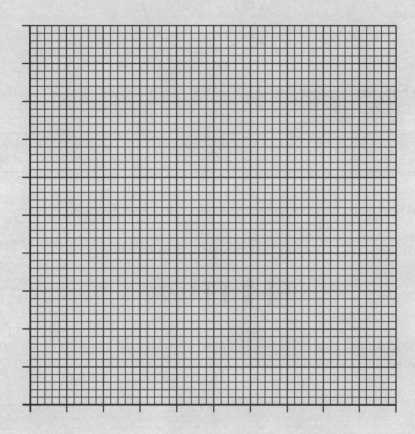

2

(*c*) The experiment was repeated using the same volume of hydrochloric acid, but with a concentration of 2 mol/l.

What mass loss would have been recorded?

_____ g

1

(*d*) Name the salt produced when marble chips react with hydrochloric acid.

_____

1

(5)

[Turn over

Marks | KU | PS

13. In a hydrogen molecule the atoms share two electrons in a covalent bond.

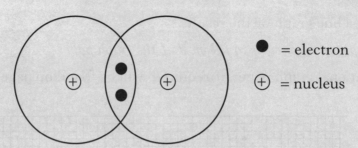

● = electron

⊕ = nucleus

(a) Explain how the covalent bond holds the two hydrogen atoms together.

_____

_____

_____

1

(b) The hydrogen molecule can be represented more simply as

$$H \!:\! H$$

(i) Showing **all** outer electrons, draw a similar diagram to represent a molecule of ammonia, NH_3.

1

(ii) Draw another diagram to show the **shape** of an ammonia molecule.

1

(3)

Marks | KU | PS

14. Methanol can take part in many chemical reactions.

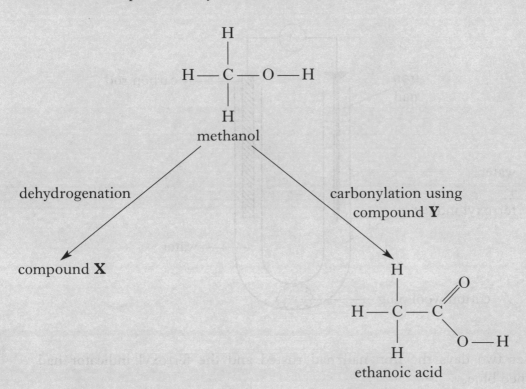

(a) (i) Compound **X** has the molecular formula CH_2O.

Draw the full structural formula for compound **X**.

1

(ii) Methanol is changed to compound **X** by dehydrogenation.

Suggest what is meant by **dehydrogenation**.

_____

_____

_____

1

(b) In carbonylation, methanol reacts with compound **Y** forming only ethanoic acid.

Suggest a name for compound **Y**.

_____

1

(3)

DO NOT
WRITE IN
THIS
MARGIN

Marks | KU | PS

15. Gemma and Laura set up the simple cell shown below.

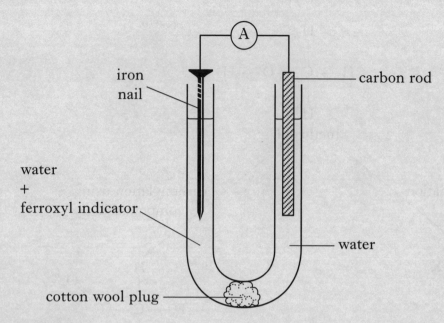

iron nail

carbon rod

water + ferroxyl indicator

water

cotton wool plug

After two days the iron nail had rusted and the ferroxyl indicator had turned blue.

(a) **On the diagram**, clearly mark the path and direction of electron flow.

1

(b) The reaction taking place at the carbon rod produces hydroxide ions.

How could Gemma and Laura have shown that hydroxide ions were present?

_____

_____

1

(2)

Marks KU PS

16. Electrolysis is a common industrial process. Some uses of electrolysis are shown in the diagram.

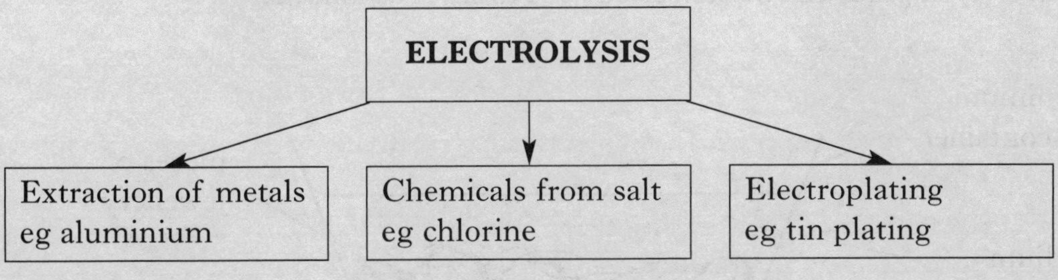

```
        ┌─────────────────────┐
        │     ELECTROLYSIS     │
        └─────────────────────┘
```

| Extraction of metals eg aluminium | Chemicals from salt eg chlorine | Electroplating eg tin plating |

(a) State what is meant by electrolysis.

_____

_____

_____   **1**

(b) Aluminium is extracted by electrolysis of its molten oxide since aluminium oxide does not react when heated with carbon.
Why does aluminium oxide **not** react with hot carbon?

_____

_____

_____   **1**

(c) Chlorine is produced by the electrolysis of sodium chloride solution.
Write the ion-electron equation for the formation of chlorine.
You may wish to use the data booklet to help you.

_____   **1**

(d) Tin plated iron rusts very rapidly if the plating is scratched.
Explain why the iron rusts so rapidly.

_____

_____

_____   **2**

(5)

[Turn over

Marks | KU | PS

17. Silver jewellery slowly tarnishes in air. This is due to the formation of silver(I) sulphide, Ag_2S.

The silver(I) sulphide can be converted back to silver as follows.

aluminium
foil container

pieces of
jewellery

sodium
hydrogencarbonate
solution

(a) Write the ionic formula for sodium hydrogencarbonate.
You may wish to use the data booklet to help you.

_____

1

(b) The equation for the reaction which takes place in the aluminium container is:

$$Ag_2S \quad + \quad Al \quad \rightarrow \quad Ag \quad + \quad Al_2S_3$$

(i) Balance this equation.

1

(ii) Name the type of chemical reaction which takes place.

_____

1

(c) Calculate the percentage by mass of aluminium in Al_2S_3.
Show your working clearly.

2

(5)

Marks | KU | PS

18. Fritz was investigating the properties of ammonia.

Before   **After**

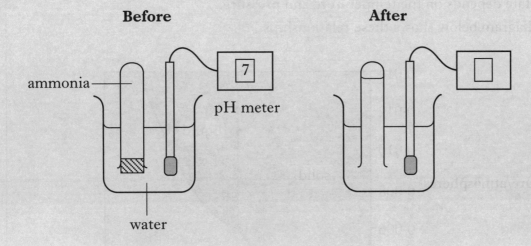

(a) Why did the water rise up the test tube when the stopper was removed?

_____

_____   1

(b) When the stopper was removed the reading on the pH meter changed. Suggest what the new reading would have been.

_____   1

       (2)

[Turn over

Marks KU PS

19. Water can exist in three different states: solid, liquid and gas.

The state depends on the temperature and pressure.

The diagram below shows these relationships.

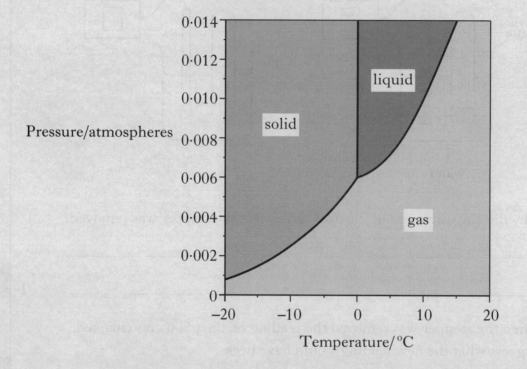

(a) In which state would water exist at 15 °C and 0·007 atmospheres?

_____

1

(b) Solid water at 0·004 atmospheres is allowed to warm up. The pressure is kept constant.

At what temperature would the solid water change into a gas?

_____ °C

1

(2)

Marks KU PS

20. Dienes are a homologous series of hydrocarbons which contain two double bonds per molecule.

buta-1,3-diene

penta-1,3-diene

hexa-1,3-diene

(a) What is meant by the term "homologous series"?

_____

_____

_____   1

(b) Suggest a general formula for the dienes.

_____   1

(c) Write the **molecular formula** for the product of the complete reaction of penta-1,3-diene with bromine.

_____   1

(d) Draw a full structural formula for an isomer of buta-1,3-diene which contains only **one** double bond per molecule.

1

(4)

Marks | KU | PS

21. A pupil carried out a titration using the chemicals and apparatus shown below.

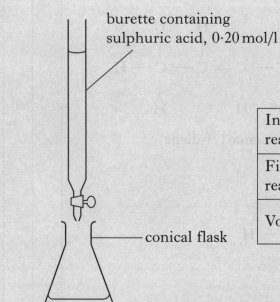

burette containing
sulphuric acid, 0·20 mol/l

conical flask

	Rough titre	**1st titre**	**2nd titre**
Initial burette reading/cm³	0·5	21·7	0·3
Final burette reading/cm³	21·7	42·4	20·8
Volume used/cm³	21·2	20·7	20·5

20 cm³ potassium hydroxide solution + indicator

(*a*) How would the pupil know when to stop adding acid from the burette?

_____

_____ 1

(*b*) (i) What average volume should be used to calculate the number of moles of sulphuric acid needed to neutralise the potassium hydroxide solution?

_____ cm³ 1

Marks KU PS

21. **(b)** **(continued)**

(ii) Calculate the number of moles of sulphuric acid in this average volume.

Show your working clearly.

_____ mol   1

(iii) The equation for the titration reaction is

$$H_2SO_4 \quad + \quad 2KOH \quad \rightarrow \quad K_2SO_4 \quad + \quad 2H_2O$$

Calculate the number of moles of potassium hydroxide in $20\,cm^3$ of the potassium hydroxide solution.

Show your working clearly.

_____ mol   1

                                                         (4)

[END OF QUESTION PAPER]

ADDITIONAL SPACE FOR ANSWERS

ADDITIONAL GRAPH PAPER FOR QUESTION 12(*b*)

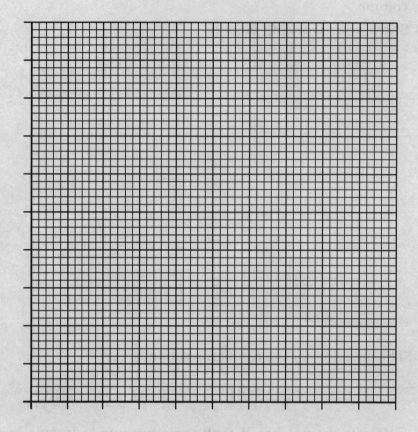

ADDITIONAL SPACE FOR ANSWERS

DO NOT
WRITE IN
THIS
MARGIN

KU	PS

ADDITIONAL SPACE FOR ANSWERS